DISCOVERING ANCIENT TECHNOLOGY

DISCOVERING THE TECHNOLOGY OF THE ANCIENT AMERICAS

LINDSEY LOWE

Cavendish Square

Published in 2024 by Cavendish Square Publishing, LLC
2544 Clinton Street, Buffalo, NY 14224

Portions of this work were originally authored by Charlie Samuels and published as *Technology in the Ancient Americas*. All new material this edition authored by Lindsey Lowe.

Website: cavendishsq.com

Children's Publisher: Anne O'Daly
Design Manager: Keith Davis
Designer: Lynne Lennon
Picture Manager: Sophie Mortimer

Picture Credits
Front Cover: Shutterstock: Gimas br, Guzel Studio t.
iStock: 18, Hiking Photographer 12, Andy Krakovski 32; Library of Congress: 5; Public Domain: Brooklyn Museum/John Thomas Underwood Memorial Fund 41, Ethnological Museum, Berlin/FA2010 34, Gary Todd 20, Walters Art Museum 42; Shutterstock: Paulo Afonso 6, Freancesco Dazzi 24, Herbert Eisengruber 37, Everett Collection 39, Amy Nichole Harris 29, Pablo Hidalgo 25, Irafael 30, Kenneth Keifer 17, Tomaz Kunst 22, W. Scott McGill 36, Dave Rock 33, Porco Rosso 35, Joel Shawn 11, slowmotiongli 38, zimmytws 31; Thinkstock/istockphoto: 1, 7, 9, 10, 14, 16, 26, 28, 40; Top Photo Group 4.

Cataloging-in-Publication Data

Names: Lowe, Lindsey.
Title: Discovering the technology of ancient Americas / Lindsey Lowe.
Description: Buffalo, New York : Cavendish Square Publishing, 2024. |
Series: Discovering ancient technology | Includes glossary and index.
Identifiers: ISBN 9781502669308 (pbk.) | ISBN 9781502669315 (library bound) |
ISBN 9781502669322 (ebook)
Subjects: LCSH: America--Civilization--Juvenile literature.
Classification: LCC T16.L69 2024 | DDC 970--dc23

CPSIA compliance information: Batch #CSCSQ24: For further information contact Cavendish Square Publishing LLC at 1-877-980-4450.

Printed in the United States of America

CONTENTS

INTRODUCTION 4
TECHNICAL KNOW-HOW 6
FARMING 8
INCA TERRACES AND IRRIGATION 10
MOUND BUILDERS 12
ZIGGURATS AND PYRAMIDS 14
CLIFF HOUSES 16
PUEBLO BUILDING 18
TENOCHTITLÁN 20
NAZCA LINES 22
TRANSPORTATION 24
INCA ROADS AND BRIDGES 26
ASTRONOMY 28
CALENDARS 30
WRITING SYSTEM 32
METALWORK 34
WARFARE AND WEAPONS 36
MEDICINE 38
TEXTILES 40
POTTERY 42
TIMELINE 44

GLOSSARY 46
FURTHER RESOURCES 47
INDEX 48

INTRODUCTION

The Maya built this tomb for King Pakal in the city of Palenque in southern Mexico during the seventh century C.E.

The peoples of the ancient Americas had developed sophisticated cultures many centuries before the arrival of the Europeans. When the first Spaniards arrived early in the 16th century, they were amazed by the cities of the Aztec and Inca. Many early Americans left little evidence of their existence, but in the deserts of what is now the U.S. Southwest, in the jungles of Mesoamerica (southern Mexico and Central America), and in the Andes Mountains, people achieved high levels of craftsmanship. Innovation helped them adapt to what were often hostile environments, and their technology gradually changed in a series of tiny steps over time, rather than in great leaps.

THREE MIGHTY EMPIRES

This book covers a period from about 1000 B.C.E. to about C.E. 1550. It concentrates on the empires of the Maya and Aztec of Mexico, and the Inca of Peru. The Maya Empire had fallen into decline by the 10th century C.E. The later empires of the Aztec and Inca lasted until the Spaniards arrived in Mexico in 1519 and in Peru in 1532. Weakened by political division and facing superior weapons, these empires also eventually fell. This book introduces examples of the remarkable technology that existed in the Americas before the arrival of the Europeans.

The Spaniards were shocked by Aztec human sacrifice. Victims were killed on top of high pyramids and their bodies were then thrown off.

TECHNICAL KNOW-HOW

Before the great Aztec and Inca empires arose in the 15th and 16th centuries, other civilizations had achieved high levels of technological accomplishment. They included the Maya, whose culture began as early as 1500 B.C.E., but which had largely vanished by the mid-ninth century C.E.

The Aztec and Inca drew on the technology of these earlier peoples. For example, the Aztec adapted the Mayan calendar and forms of Mayan writing.

The Olmec carved huge heads in rock. The heads may represent people who played a sacred ball game.

OLMEC, TOLTEC, AND MOCHE

The Olmec of Mexico (1200 B.C.E.– C.E. 400) built large earth mounds to serve as ceremonial centers. They transported huge boulders without any wheeled transport, probably by using rafts on lakes and rivers. Later peoples built stone pyramids instead of mounds. The Toltec (C.E. 900–1200) built their capital city of Tula in central Mexico around a stepped temple pyramid. They also built huge basalt statues, known as Chac Mools. The Moche of Peru flourished between the second and eighth centuries C.E.. They grew crops, and built canals to irrigate them. They traveled in reed boats. Such technology was also used later by the Aztec and Inca.

The pyramids of Teotihuacán in Mexico date from the first century C.E. Over 1,400 years later, the Aztec believed they had been built by the gods.

FARMING

HARVESTING CORN

Farms allowed the early hunter-gatherer peoples of Mesoamerica to establish permanent settlements. Farming methods advanced. By the time the Spaniards arrived, the Mesoamericans were growing food that was later introduced to the rest of the world, such as the potato. Corn, the most important crop, was used as food and to make beer.

How people farmed depended on where they lived. In the highlands, the Inca used terracing to farm on the steep mountainsides. In the Mexican lowlands, the Aztec reclaimed land from swamps and lakes by making chinampas. These were built-up beds of fertile earth on top of a base of reeds. They planted seeds using a digging stick, or *uictli*.

MAYA FARMING

The Maya built drainage canals in the Yucatán and made raised beds like the Aztec chinampas. They turned the soil with digging sticks and stone-bladed hoes. They planted corn (maize) on the ridges in the soil, with beans and squash in the furrows in between the ridges.

TECHNICAL SPECS

» None of the Mesoamerican cultures used plows. Farmers turned the soil with digging sticks made from strong wood.

» The Aztec had no draft animals. They relied on human labor.

» The Maya learned to boil corn with lime or ground-up snail shells; otherwise niacin, a chemical in the corn, would cause a vitamin deficiency called pellagra.

» The Inca preserved potatoes by freezing them. They left the potatoes out overnight in the cold mountains. During the day, when the potatoes thawed, they walked on them to squeeze out moisture. After a few days, the potatoes (or *chuño*) were ready to be stored for up to a year.

The American peoples bred many different varieties of corn, which grew even at high altitudes in the Andes.

INCA TERRACES AND IRRIGATION

The Inca lived high up in the Andes. The ground was very steep and the soil was poor. The Inca dug flat terraces and water channels so they could grow crops on the mountainside. Other American peoples also built canals for irrigation.

These narrow terraces were built by the Inca at the city of Machu Picchu, high in the Andes mountains.

The Inca diverted rivers such as the Urubamba to water fields in the few flat-floored valleys.

The Inca dug steps into the mountainside. The steps were supported with stone walls. As well as creating more land for crops, the terraces helped to prevent erosion of the soil by wind or rain.

IRRIGATION CANALS

To water the terraces, the Inca built canals along the contours of the slopes. In North America, the Hohokam of the Sonoran Desert (C.E. 200–1400) also built canals to irrigate their fields. They used dams to control the flow of the water from the Gila River.

TECHNICAL SPECS

» At the peak of the Inca Empire in the 16th century C.E., terraces covered 3,860 square miles (10,000 sq km).

» The stone retaining walls helped keep the soil warm during cold nights. This helped extend the growing season.

» Inca terraces conserved water well. The soil stayed damp for six months after rain.

» The Inca mixed the soil with small stones, otherwise the soil would have expanded after rain and pushed out the retaining wall.

» The Inca made mortar to build canals from a mixture of cement, lime, sand, and water.

MOUND BUILDERS

Serpent Mound may have had an astrological purpose. It seems to align with the position of the sun on important days of the year.

Farming peoples had settled in parts of North America by 1000 B.C.E. They grew crops as well as continuing to gather wild plants. Some of these peoples built huge earthworks. These were probably used as tombs or for ceremonial purposes. Mound building continued in North American settlements for about 2,000 years.

CAHOKIA

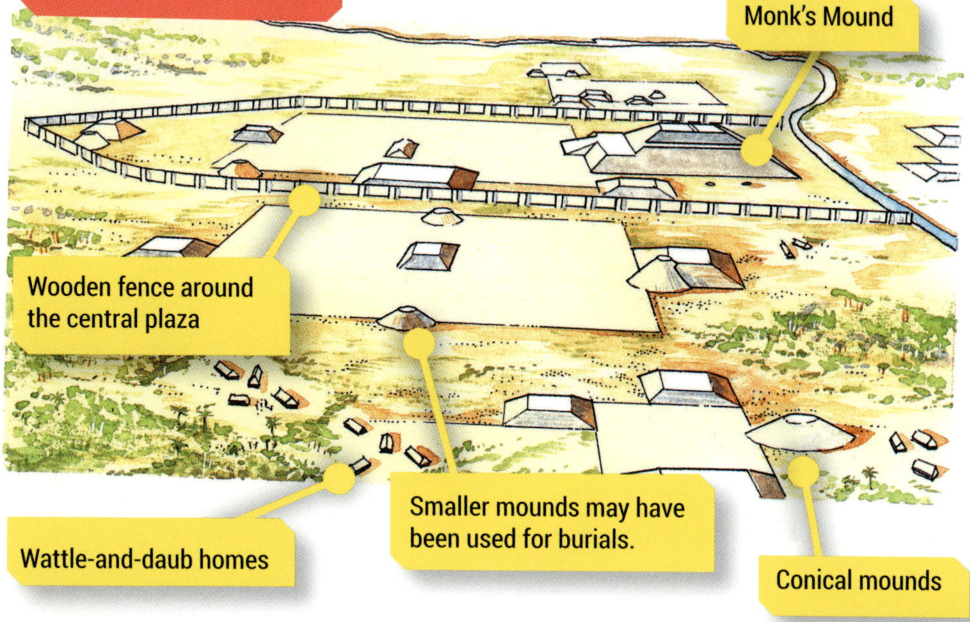

Around 10,000 people lived in the settlement of Cahokia (present-day Missouri). At its peak in about C.E. 1100, Cahokia had more than 100 mounds. The largest is Monk's Mound, a flat-topped structure with four terraces. At Emerald Mound in Mississippi, the Natchez people flattened a hill to make a large platform.

SERPENT MOUND

A mound was built in what is now Ohio in about C.E. 1070. It was shaped like a long serpent and followed the natural curves of the land. It may have had astronomical meaning. Its coils align with the equinoxes and solstices.

TECHNICAL SPECS

» The mound builders had no carts or pack animals. They had to carry the earth in baskets.

» Monk's Mound at Cahokia contains about 780,000 cubic yards (600,000 cu m) of earth.

» Two flat-topped earth pyramids stood on the platform on top of Emerald Mound. The larger was almost 33 feet (10 m) tall.

» If the Serpent Mound was built in C.E. 1070, it may have marked two astronomical events: the explosion of a supernova in 1054 and the coming of Halley's Comet in 1066.

ZIGGURATS AND PYRAMIDS

The Maya built this pyramid at Chichén Itzá between the 9th and 12th centuries C.E. in honor of the god Kukulkán.

Mesoamerican peoples began to build stepped pyramids, or ziggurats, thousands of years after the Egyptians built their great pyramids. Although they were similar to Egyptian pyramids in some ways, the American structures had flat tops and flights of steps that led up to a temple at the top.

AMERICAN PYRAMIDS

The Olmec built the earliest pyramid in the Americas in about 900 B.C.E. at La Venta. Later, the Maya built pyramids from stone blocks that had steep steps up the outside. The pyramids had temples at the top. In Teotihuacán, in Mexico, the Pyramid of the Sun and the Pyramid of the Moon were built in the first century C.E. They stood on an avenue lined by smaller structures. The Aztec built pyramids in the heart of their capital, Tenochtitlán. Priests used altars on top of the pyramids to sacrifice prisoners to the gods.

TECHNICAL SPECS

» Olmec pyramids represented the sacred mountain the Olmec believed reached up to heaven.

» The Maya city of Tikal had six tall pyramids, each with a temple on top.

» Mayan pyramids represented the three levels of the Maya universe: the underworld, the earthly world, and the heavenly world.

» At Teotihuacán, human sacrifices were buried in the foundations of the Pyramid of the Moon.

» The Pyramid of the Sun at Teotihuacán was 210 feet (64 m) tall; its base measured 720 by 760 feet (220 by 232 m).

TEOTIHUACÁN

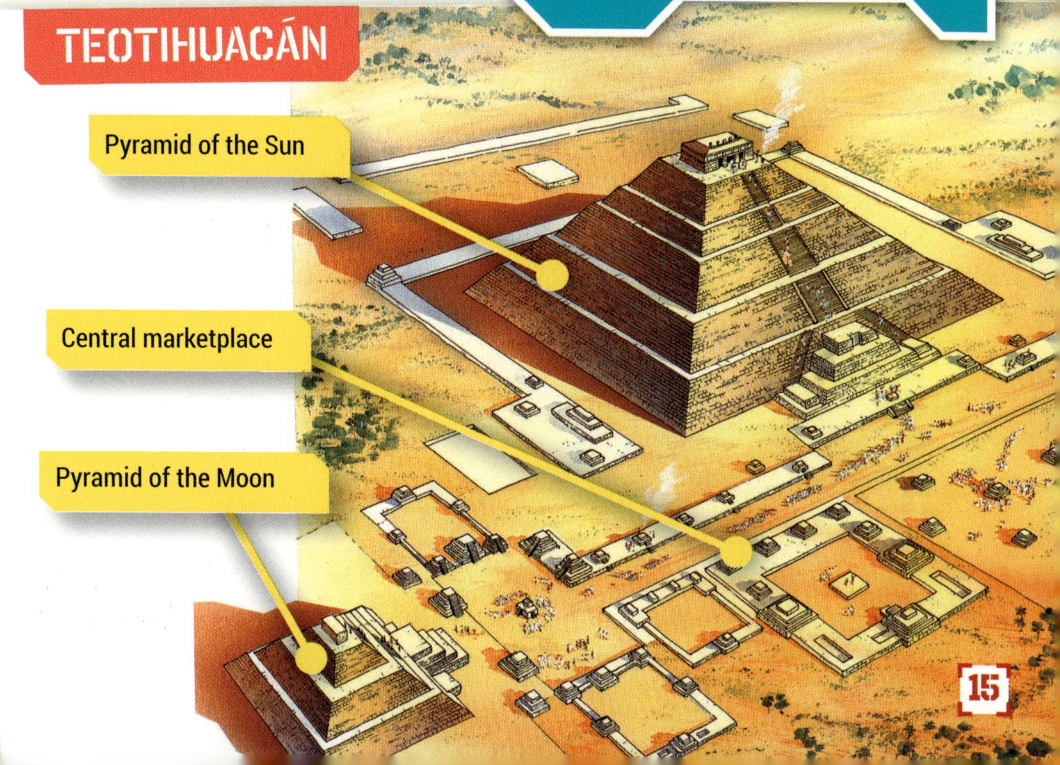

CLIFF HOUSES

In around the sixth century C.E., the formerly nomadic Anasazi settled in communities in the Southwest of North America. This was the region now known as the Four Corners, where Colorado, Arizona, New Mexico, and Utah meet. They built their homes high up on the cliffs for protection. Their descendants are the Ancestral Puebloans.

Beneath a cliff in Canyon de Chelly, Arizona, the White House was home to a whole Anasazi community.

The Cliff Palace at Mesa Verde is sheltered beneath a cliff. The round structures are ceremonial rooms named kivas.

The early Anasazi lived in homes made from adobe, or mud brick. Some were partly dug into the ground. By the 13th century C.E., they lived in stone houses up to four stories high. The houses had no windows or doors on the ground floor. Ladders led to entrances in the roof.

HOMES ON CLIFFS

At Mesa Verde, the Anasazi built homes in shallow caves and overhangs in cliff faces. The houses were accessed by ladders. The builders had no metal tools. They shaped sandstone blocks for building by chipping them with harder stones from nearby riverbeds.

TECHNICAL SPECS

» Adobe bricks were made of sand, clay, and water mixed with straw. The mixture was shaped using frames and dried in the sun.

» The Anasazi are known as the "basketmakers" because they used baskets to cook in instead of clay or metal cooking pots.

» At Chaco Canyon, the "great house" at Pueblo Bonito had as many as 800 rooms.

» At Mesa Verde, some ancient sites are high on cliffs. The Anasazi probably climbed to them using rope ladders or footholds carved into the rock.

PUEBLOS

Taos Pueblo, New Mexico, was built by the Taos people over 1,000 years ago. It has been lived in ever since.

Peoples in the ancient Americas built their homes using materials that were easily available. The Aztec and Maya used stone for public buildings such as temples and palaces. In the lowlands of Mesoamerica and the deserts of the Southwest, it rarely rains. Mud brick, or adobe, was the main building material.

The Aztec built single-story homes using adobe bricks made from sun-dried mud and straw. The houses had one big room with a roof of thatched straw.

PUEBLO PEOPLES

To the north, the Pueblo peoples were influenced by techniques from Mexico. The Anasazi built large structures with many homes. The largest housed thousands of people. Access was gained by ladders leading to doorways on the flat roofs. Circular pits named kivas were dug into the ground. They were used for ceremonies.

TECHNICAL SPECS

» The Aztec wove reed mats to sleep on the floor and built reed chests for clothes. The Inca had no furniture.

» The Maya made plaster to line their pueblo homes by burning limestone for 36 hours to make a powder. The powder was mixed with water to make plaster.

» Pueblo Bonito's original gateway was narrowed and then blocked completely.

» The lower rooms in the pueblo had no windows. They were probably used for storage.

HOW TO ...

Pueblo Bonito was the largest settlement in Chaco Canyon, New Mexico. It was built in a large D-shape, with its curved back facing the canyon wall, and could only be entered by ladder. It contained at least 800 joined rooms, which were built on several levels. It probably housed as many as 1,200 people at its height in the 12th century C.E.

TENOCHTITLÁN

This painting shows the ceremonial center of Tenochtitlán, and the causeways linking it to the shores of Lake Texcoco.

In C.E. 1519, Spanish conquerors arrived in the Aztec capital of Tenochtitlán. They could not believe their eyes. The city was laid out in a grid pattern and had been built on swampy islands on Lake Texcoco, in the Valley of Mexico. It was more sophisticated and larger than any European city.

To build on the swampy land, the Aztecs created chinampas. These were mounds of mud from the lake that were piled on top of reeds and mats weighted with stones and sunk between poles.

CITY ON AN ISLAND

The Aztec built two terracotta clay aqueducts to carry fresh water across to the island. The island was accessed by three causeways. Only the center of the island was strong enough to support any stone structures. The main temples and palaces were located on this spot. Ordinary people lived in one-room, one-story adobe buildings.

TECHNICAL SPECS

» The causeways had bridges in the middle that could be pulled up to defend the city.

» People used flat-bottomed canoes to travel around the city's canals.

» The Spaniards claimed that the causeways were wide enough for 10 horses to walk side by side.

» The Templo Mayor in the heart of the city was rebuilt seven times. Each temple was built on top of the last. Its weight made it sink into the mud of Lake Texcoco.

» Modern-day Mexico City is built on the foundations of Tenochtitlán.

» The Aztec used human waste from public toilets to fertilize crops.

CENTER OF THE CITY

NAZCA LINES

This design is known as the hummingbird. Other images showed a whale and a monkey.

The Nazca culture existed in southern Peru between 100 B.C.E. and C.E. 800. The Nazca people are best known for drawing huge images and miles of lines on the stony desert floor. No one really knows why they were drawn. Scientists have tried to work out how they were made.

HOW TO ...

The Nazca Lines cover an area of 190 square miles (500 sq km); the longest is over 5 miles (8 km) long. Some align with the setting sun on important days such as the winter solstice, the shortest day of the year (December 21). The builders may have plotted the lines from nearby hills, as the shapes are impossible to make out from ground level.

UNEXPLAINED

The huge drawings created in the desert show geometric shapes and lines, but also animals, birds, flowers, and trees. The lines were made by removing the reddish pebbles from the desert floor to uncover the whitish ground beneath. The lines have been preserved for centuries in the dry conditions. They may have been planned by studying the ground from low foothills nearby. After many centuries, the reason for their existence remains a mystery. Some people have even claimed that they were intended to guide alien spaceships to Earth.

TECHNICAL SPECS

» The Nazca Lines cover 190 square miles (500 sq km) of the Nazca desert, which is one of the driest places in the world.

» Creating the lines revealed a sublayer of soil that contains high levels of lime. The lime hardened in the sun's heat, helping to preserve the lines.

» The largest shape is 660 feet (200 m) across. For centuries it was thought the shapes could only be seen from the air, but they can also be seen clearly from the nearby hilltops.

» The Nazca Lines were probably carved using simple tools such as wooden stakes.

TRANSPORTATION

Although the Aztec, Inca, and Maya made wheeled toys, they did not use wheels for transportation. Wheeled vehicles would have been of limited use in the mountains or forests, and before the arrival of the Spanish, there were no horses to pull carts. Most journeys were made on foot or by boat.

Reed boats known as balsa are still used on Lake Titicaca, in the highlands of modern-day Bolivia.

Llamas were used by the Inca for carrying loads. They also provided wool, which was woven into clothes and blankets.

The Maya and Aztec made canoes from hollowed-out tree trunks. In the Aztec capital, Tenochtitlán, the island city was crisscrossed by canals that were crowded with canoes. Families moored canoes behind their homes.

REED BOATS

Timber was in short supply, so boats were often made from reeds that grew around lakes. They were trimmed and bound into tight bundles that were tied together to form a boat. The reeds meant the boats were light and strong. They were shaped so that each end was curved to help it move forward through the water more easily. Another form of transportation was the llama. The Inca used the llamas to carry heavy loads up the steep mountainsides.

TECHNICAL SPECS

» Larger reed boats were up to 20 feet (6 m) long. They had wooden masts and reed sails.

» In 1947 the Norwegian Thor Heyerdahl crossed the Pacific Ocean in a reed raft based on Inca designs. He believed ancient South Americans traded with the islands of the South Pacific.

» The Aztec used wheels on toys, but not on vehicles.

» The Inca prized llamas so highly they did not eat them for meat.

INCA ROADS AND BRIDGES

Inca roads used shallow steps to climb up hillsides; on steeper slopes, the roads zigzagged back and forth.

The imperial city of Cusco was the heart of the Inca Empire. Every road led directly to Cusco. The Inca were master builders and, oddly for a civilization that never used the wheel, they created an extensive road system. They built roads up steep mountainsides and constructed bridges across deep valleys.

COMMUNICATIONS

The two main road systems ran from north to south. El Camino de la Costa ran along the Pacific Ocean for 2,500 miles (4,000 km). Inland, the Camino Real, or Royal Way, ran through the Andes from Ecuador south to Argentina, via Cusco. The two roads were linked by smaller roads. Couriers (*chasquis*) ran in relays with messages to and from Cusco. The Inca army also used the roads to march to the corners of the empire. Ordinary people were not allowed to use them. Where the terrain was interrupted by canyons, the Inca built rope suspension bridges.

TECHNICAL SPECS

» The Camino Real was made from flat stones, while the coastal road was paved with clay bricks.

» The coastal road was up to 15 feet (5 m) wide. The mountain road was narrower. It followed the contours of the landscape.

» Royal messengers could cover 200 miles (320 km) a day.

» On steep mountainsides, roads zigzagged or went up stone steps.

» Branches were braided between cables to form a bridge. Two more cables acted as guardrails.

» The bridge across Apurimac Canyon on the Camino Real was 120 feet (36 m) above a river.

Inca roads crossed deep ravines over suspension bridges made from cables of twisted plant fiber.

ASTRONOMY

The Maya believed their gods lived in the sky. The Aztec and Inca also watched the skies. Their astronomers noted the cycles of heavenly events. The ancient Americans based their lives on interpreting what they saw in the sky. The sun and moon played an important role in everyday life, ceremonies, and rituals.

El Caracol at Chichén Itzá was used to study the heavens. It was aligned with the movements of Venus.

Machu Picchu was a sacred Inca city where priests performed ceremonies dedicated to the sun.

The Maya used the cycles of the sun and moon to predict the future. Priests told rulers the best times for actions, such as going to war. The Maya also studied the planets, particularly Venus and Mars. They had the most advanced calendar of the ancient Americans.

SOLSTICES

Like the Maya, the Aztec aligned their temples and pyramids with the summer and winter solstices. The Inca also worked out the time of the solstices. It helped them know when to plant crops.

TECHNICAL SPECS

» The Aztec built the chief pyramids in Tenochtitlán so the sun's rays passed between them on the spring equinox, March 21.

» The Maya worked out that a lunar month is 29.5302 days long. The precise length is 29.53059 days.

» The Maya could predict solar eclipses, but not where they could be seen.

» The Hitching Post of the Sun at Machu Picchu indicated the two equinoxes. The sun was directly above the stone pillar on March 21 and September 23, so it cast almost no shadow.

CALENDARS

This Maya stone carving is a representation of the calendar used for "long counts."

In December 2012, the Maya hit the news headlines. People across the world waited to see if the world would end on December 21, as had been predicted by the Mayan calendar. Fortunately, this prediction was wrong. However, the calendar was mostly extremely accurate, and was used by other Mesoamerican civilizations.

COMPLEX CALENDARS

There were three Mayan calendars. The first was based on a sacred year of 260 days. It had two different simultaneous weeks: a numbered week of 13 days and a named week of 20 days. The second calendar was based on the solar year, and was used by farmers. It had 18 months of 20 days, with five unlucky extra days to make a year of 365 days. A third calendar was used for "long counts" made up of cycles. The longest cycle was an "alautun" of 23,040,000,000 days. Both the Maya and Aztec believed the end of a cycle was an unlucky time.

TECHNICAL SPECS

» The Maya believed that anyone born on one of the five unlucky days was cursed.

» The Mayan calendar began on August 13, 3114 B.C.E. No one knows why they chose that date.

» The Maya and Aztec thought cycles followed each other.

» The sacred calendar had two wheels, one with 13 numbers and the other with 20 named days. The wheels turned to match a number with a day. The whole cycle took 260 days.

» At the end of a cycle, the Aztec let all their fires go out. A human sacrifice was made and his heart removed. A priest lit a fire inside his empty chest that was used to relight all the other fires.

In this carving of the solar calendar, the Mayan god of time is surrounded by the names of the months.

WRITING SYSTEM

The Maya and the Aztec developed a system of writing using hieroglyphics. The characters were carved in stone or written on paper made from the bark of fig trees. Counting systems using base 20 were also developed. The Inca did not use a writing system. Instead, they kept records and communicated using quipu, which were colored knotted strings.

Individual strings were tied onto a cord. Experts are still learning about them today.

Mayan writing was carved into stone for sacred purposes and to record important dates and events.

Mayan writing had around 850 hieroglyphs. It was difficult to read. Each symbol stood for a word or part of a word, but could also stand for an idea or a sound. The Maya wrote on stone and in books called codices. The Aztec also used hieroglyphs, but few people were able to read. Both the Maya and the Aztec used symbols for numbers.

INCA QUIPU

Inca quipu were knotted strings of various thicknesses and colors. The information recorded varied according to the type of knot, the color, and position of the strings.

TECHNICAL SPECS

» The paper used in codices was made from the fibers of the bark of fig trees. The folded pages were bound in animal skin.

» The Maya wrote in codices using fine brushes of animal hair. They kept ink in conch shells cut in half. Four codices still exist.

» Quipu were used to keep records of taxes, population numbers, and business deals.

» Quipu were created and read by trained accountants. Some quipu had more than 2,000 strings.

» To show something was further away, the Aztec drew a glyph closer to the top of a page.

» Mayan number symbols were arranged on three lines.

METALWORK

When the Spanish conquerors arrived in the Inca capital at Cusco, they could not believe their eyes. Gold and silver were everywhere. Ancient peoples in Peru started to make objects out of gold 3,000 years ago. The Moche of northern Peru were probably the first to cast metal, in around C.E. 100.

Gold and silver were in plentiful supply in Peru. Metals were collected by sifting river gravel in trays. Flecks of metal were easy to spot. The Inca also dug out shallow gold and silver mines.

This gold figure was the handle of an Inca knife used to sacrifice animals in religious rituals.

TECHNICAL SPECS

» The Moche developed a method of adding a thin layer of gold—gold plate—to copper. They dissolved gold in acid, then placed a copper object in the liquid. Gold coated the copper and was heated to make it bind permanently.

» The Inca called gold "the sweat of the sun" and silver "the tears of the moon."

» Inca and Mesoamerican smiths used gold, silver, and copper, with some tin, lead, and platinum. They did not use iron.

» The earliest known goldwork was made in Peru around 3,000 years ago.

» The Inca smelted metals in clay furnaces with holes in the front to allow a flow of air to raise the heat of the fire enough to melt metals.

This figurine was made by the Inca. It is similar to other miniature figurines that were often used in sacred rituals.

SPREADING SKILLS

The Moche were skilled metalworkers. They cast objects by pouring molten metal into molds. The technique spread north, reaching Mesoamerica in about C.E. 900.

GOLD WORKERS

Goldsmiths were important members of Aztec society. They cast objects using the "lost wax" method. The Inca cast gold and also used cold working. This involved beating the gold into thin sheets that could then be shaped and soldered together to form hollow objects.

WARFARE AND WEAPONS

The Aztec, Inca, and Maya were warring peoples. Astronomy and religion were major causes of conflict. Peoples expanded their territory by going to war against their neighbors. Another important reason to go to war was to capture prisoners for sacrifice to keep the gods happy. Warriors were important people in their societies.

This clay model of a warrior was made in around C.E. 600 by the Zapotec people who lived in Mexico.

All Mesoamerican males served in the army from the age of 17. Weapons were wooden clubs and spears tipped with obsidian (Aztec) or bronze (Inca).

This carving shows a Mayan warrior in a helmet decorated with feathers. Feathers were a symbol of high status.

The Inca used slingshots made from hide or wood to throw rocks. They also threw bolas, which were leather straps with rocks tied at the ends. When thrown at an enemy, they wrapped around his legs and tripped him up.

ARMOR AND SHIELDS

Warriors wore quilted cotton tunics and wooden armor. Most shields and helmets were made from wood, but the Aztec made shields from jaguar skin and brightly colored tropical feathers.

TECHNICAL SPECS

» Aztec warriors carried a wooden *maquahuitl* or war club. It was 30 inches (76 cm) long and had grooved sides set with obsidian stone blades.

» The atlatl helped the warrior to throw spears over 300 feet (100 m). It was a wooden shaft with a handle on one end and a cup on the other, into which the end of the spear fitted.

» Flint was used to make sharp knives.

» Despite being well trained and large, both the Inca and Aztec armies were easily defeated by a tiny number of Spaniards. The invaders had guns, steel swords, and horses, which the Inca and Aztec had never seen before.

MEDICINE

In the ancient Americas, people thought it was the gods who made them sick. Healers called upon the gods for help, but they also understood certain things about the workings of the human body. They used plants as medicine to cure ailments. Cures were a mixture of magic, offerings to please the gods, and practical medicine.

A coca plantation in South America. Coca has been used for medicinal purposes in the region for centuries.

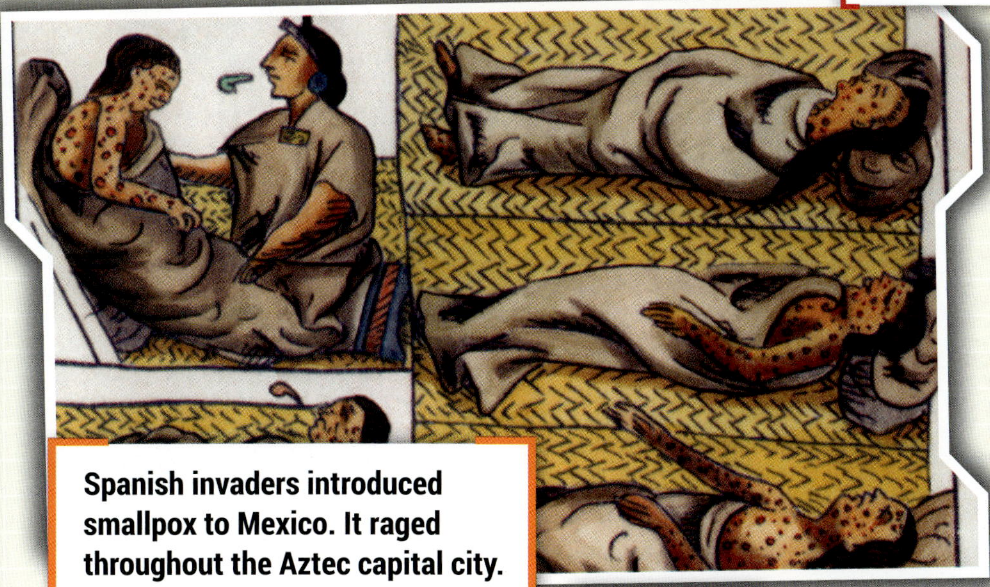

Spanish invaders introduced smallpox to Mexico. It raged throughout the Aztec capital city.

The Aztec and the Inca performed surgery with knives made from flint or obsidian. They stitched wounds with human hair or vegetable fibers, using needles made from bone. Inca surgeons bored holes in skulls to relieve headaches and could amputate limbs if necessary.

REMEDIES AND PREVENTION

The Aztec used plants as remedies. They thought tobacco cleared the head and coca plants deadened pain. They grew medicinal plants in special botanical gardens. The Aztec took good care of their mouths. After eating, they rinsed their mouths with water and used thorns as toothpicks.

TECHNICAL SPECS

» Broken limbs were mended by joining the broken ends of a bone together. A poultice of plant root was applied and the limb was held in place by wooden splints bound with cords.

» Tartar was removed from teeth with charcoal and salt water, or a mixture of alum, salt, chili, and cochineal.

» The Inca chewed coca leaves to help combat altitude sickness.

» Quinine comes from a Peruvian tree. Ancient peoples used it to prevent and treat malaria; it is used for the same purpose today.

» The Spaniards brought smallpox with them. Native peoples had no immunity to it, so the disease killed millions of people.

TEXTILES

A descendant of the Inca weaves on a backstrap loom. The long threads are the warp threads.

Some of the most remarkable textiles in South America were also some of the earliest. The Paracas people, who lived in the Andes from about 900 B.C.E. to C.E. 400, wove elaborate designs into their cloth. For the Inca who followed them, textiles were their most valuable possessions. They were made from cotton, or the wool from alpacas and llamas. Textiles were more valuable than gold.

The Paracas people wove textiles from the wool of llamas and alpacas and from plant fibers, such as cotton. Designs woven into the cloth helped to preserve the tribe's religious beliefs. Some textiles are up to 115 feet (35 m) long: to produce them would have required many workers.

BACKSTRAP LOOM

Andean peoples wove on a backstrap loom. One end of the warp threads was attached to a wooden bar that was hung on a tree or post. The other end was strapped around the weaver's back. The weaver altered the tension of the yarn by leaning back as she passed the weft thread through the warp threads.

TECHNICAL SPECS

» In Paracas, cloth was dyed with bright colors such as indigo (blue) and pink.

» Paracas cloth was often heavily embroidered. It was used to wrap dead bodies before they were buried.

» One ancient Peruvian noble was buried with 300 pounds (135 kg) of cotton in his grave.

» Cochineal beetles, which live on cactus plants, were used for red dye. To make 1 pound (454 g) of dye it took 70,000 beetles.

» Llamas and alpacas produced good wool, but the finest came from their relative, the wild vicuña.

Part of "The Paracas Textile," a 2,000-year-old cloth that was used to wrap mummified bodies in Peru. It was found buried in the sand along Peru's Pacific coast.

POTTERY

The Mesoamericans and Inca did not use potter's wheels or kilns, but they were skilled potters. Every vessel was shaped by hand. The pots were richly decorated using a variety of techniques. The best ceramics were used for religious ceremonies or by rich people.

Pottery in the Andes and Mesoamerica was made by shaping coils of clay, by molding the clay, or by carving blocks of clay. Mesoamerican potters often produced slipware. Before a pot was fired, it was decorated with semiliquid clay, known as slip. Different colored slips were used to paint decorations on the pot. Instead of using kilns, early American potters fired their pots in an open fire. They made

The Moche made "portrait vessels," which showed the likenesses of people or gods. They also made animal designs.

pottery known as blackware by controlling how much oxygen the pot received as it was fired.

DISTINCTIVE POTTERY

Some of the most distinctive pottery was made by the Moche of northern Peru. They made pots in complex human and animal forms. The pots had U-shaped "stirrup" spouts. From the ninth century C.E., the Mogollon people of Arizona and New Mexico produced a distinctive black-on-white pottery, known as Mimbres. It is notable for the hand-painted decoration that often featured elaborate geometric designs.

TECHNICAL SPECS

» The Inca used molds to make basic pots such as the aryballos jar. It had a conical base, a tall flared neck, and handles on each side.

» Most Inca pottery was shiny red, with geometric patterns in red, white, and black.

» Whistling water jars were double vessels connected by hollow tubes. As water flowed from one vessel it pushed air out of the other through a whistle. Some whistling jars were made in the shape of the quetzal, a bird that was sacred to both the Aztec and the Maya.

» The Maya covered their pots with a colored plaster called stucco.

» Mimbres pots were often buried with the dead. The pots were first "killed" by having a hole punched through their base.

Mimbres potters crushed plants and rocks to make paint. They made brushes from feathers and twigs.

TIMELINE

B.C.E.

3114 The Maya calendar begins on August 13.

c.3000 Pottery is first made in the Americas, in what are now Colombia and Ecuador.

c.1150 The Olmec culture appears in Mexico.

c.900 The Olmec build the first pyramid in America at La Venta.

c.800 The Paracas culture appears in Peru; it is famed for its textiles.

c.300 The earliest stages of Mayan culture appear in Mesoamerica.

c.300 An unknown people begins building the great city of Teotihuacán in central Mexico.

c.100 The Paracas culture disappears.

C.E.

c.100 The Olmec culture in Mexico declines.

c.100 The Moche of northern Peru begin to cast objects in metal.

c.400 The Nazca of Peru begin drawing huge designs in the desert.

c.500 The Maya build the city of Tikal, which has many tall pyramids.

c.600 The Maya civilization reaches its height.

c.600 Teotihuacán is abandoned for unknown reasons.

c.600 Cahokia is founded in modern-day Missouri.

c.850 The Maya civilization begins a decline.

899 The Maya abandon the city of Tikal.

c.900 The Pueblo build adobe communal dwellings in Chaco Canyon.

c.900	Casting techniques reach Mesoamerica.
c.1000	The Mogollon culture reaches its classic phase, producing distinctive black-and-white Mimbres pottery.
c.1070	The Natchez people build Serpent Mound in Mississippi.
c.1100	The Toltec emerge in Mexico, building a capital at Tula.
c.1100	At its peak, Cahokia in Missouri has 100 mounds.
c.1100	The Anasazi build cliff homes at Mesa Verde and Canyon de Chelly.
c.1200	The Aztec move into central Mexico from an origin further to the north.
c.1200	The first Inca emperor, Manco Cápac, founds an empire from Cusco in the Andes.
1325	The Aztec begin their rise to power, and build their capital, Teotihuacán, in the middle of a shallow lake.
1438	The Inca build the sacred city of Machu Picchu in a remote mountaintop location.
c.1470	The Inca conquer the neighboring Chimu culture.
1492	Christopher Columbus crosses the Atlantic and lands on the island of Hispaniola in the Caribbean, marking European contact with the Americas.
1498	Columbus lands on mainland America.
1517	The first Spaniards land in Mexico, on the Yucatán Peninsula. They introduce illnesses, such as smallpox, to which native peoples have no immunity; within a century, these diseases devastate the population of Mesoamerica.
1519	Hernán Cortés lands in Mexico and begins to conquer the Aztec Empire.
1521	Cortés destroys the Aztec capital at Tenochtitlán; it will be rebuilt as Mexico City.

GLOSSARY

canal An artificial waterway.

cast To make objects by pouring molten metal into a mold.

causeway A raised roadway across a lake or marsh.

chinampa An artificial island built in a shallow lake for use as a "floating garden."

codices (sing. codex) Early forms of books, with pages sewn together.

embroider To sew a design onto a piece of cloth with colored thread.

empire A large territory ruled by an emperor or empress.

furnace A very hot oven used to fire clay or to melt metals.

hieroglyph A picture or symbol used for writing. Hieroglyphs can stand for things or sounds, or both.

irrigation Artificially watering fields in order to grow crops.

kiln An oven used to harden pottery or bake bricks.

"lost wax" method A way of making metal objects in which a wax model of the finished object is enclosed in a clay mold. When molten metal is poured in, the wax runs out, leaving the metal to cool and harden.

Mesoamerica An area inhabited by similar cultures that included parts of modern-day Mexico, Guatemala, Honduras, Belize, El Salvador, and Nicaragua.

nomadic A way of life in which people do not live in the same place, but move around depending on the seasons.

pueblo A communal building made of adobe in the U.S. Southwest; the term is also used to describe the peoples who built them.

pyramid A four-sided structure that tapers to a point.

slip A layer of liquid clay used to decorate pottery.

staple A food that makes up the major part of a diet.

terrace A flat bank of earth with steep sides.

ziggurat A pyramid that rises in steps to a flat top.

FURTHER RESOURCES

BOOKS

Captivating History. *Maya History for KIDS: A Captivating Guide to the Maya Civilization, from the Olmecs through the Founding of Teotihuacan in Ancient Mesoamerica to the Spanish Conquest* (History for Children). Captivating History, 2021.

Cooke, Tim. *Why were Mayan games so deadly? And other questions about the Maya* (A Question of History). Wayland, 2021.

Kule, Elaine A. *Amazing Ancients! World of the Maya.* Penguin Workshop, 2020.

Stuckey, Rachel. *Life Among the Aztec* (Ancient Americas). Rosen Publishing, 2017.

WEBSITES

www.historymuseum.ca/cmc/exhibitions/civil/maya/mmc01eng.html
Canadian Museum of Civilization introduction to the Maya: Secrets of Their World.

www.ancientworlds.net/aw/Article/729894
Ancientworlds.com guide to Inca technology, with links.

aztecs.mrdonn.org/achievements.html
Mr. Donn pages on the Aztec.

kids.britannica.com/kids/article/Aztec/352810
Britannica Kids introduction to the Aztec, with links to pages on Maya, Olmec, Toltec, and Inca.

INDEX

adobe (mud bricks) 17 18, 19
agriculture 8–9
Anasazi 16–17, 19
Andes 4, 10, 11, 27, 38, 40, 42
aqueducts 21
armor 37
astronomy 28–29
Aztec 5, 6, 11, 15, 19, 20–21, 25, 28, 29, 30, 31, 32, 33, 35, 36, 37

boats 7, 24, 25
Bolivia 24
bridges 27
building 4, 14–15, 16–17, 18–19, 20–21

Cahokia 12, 13
calendars 6, 29, 30–31
canals 11
Canyon de Chelly 16
Chaco Canyon 17, 19
Chichén Itzá 14
chinampas 11, 21
cities 20–21
codices 33
corn 10–11, 16
counting 32, 33
Cusco 26, 27, 34, 35

dyes 41

earthworks 12–13
Emerald Mound 13

farming 8–9

gold 34–35
"great houses" 17, 19

Heyerdahl, Thor 25
hieroglyphs 32, 33
Hohokam 11
homes 16–17, 18–19

Inca 5, 6, 10, 11, 26–27, 28, 29, 32, 33, 35, 36, 37, 40, 41, 43
irrigation 11

kivas 17, 19

La Venta 15
Lake Titicaca 24
llamas 25
looms 40, 41
lost wax method 35

Machu Picchu 29
Maya 4, 5, 6, 9, 14, 15, 19, 28–29, 30, 31, 32, 33, 36
medicine 38–39
Mesa Verde 17
Mesoamerica 4, 8, 35, 38, 42
metalwork 34–35
Mexico 4, 7, 15, 19
Mexico City 21
Mimbres (pottery) 43
Moche 7, 34, 35, 42, 43
Mogollon 43
Monk's Mound 13
mound building 12–13

Natchez 13
Nazca 22–23
Nazca Lines 22–23

Olmec 6, 7, 15

Palenque 4
paper 33
Paracas 40, 41
Peru 7, 22–23, 26–27, 34, 43
potato 8, 9
pottery 42–43
pueblo 18–19
Pueblo Bonito 17, 19
pyramids 5, 7, 14–15

quinine 39
quipu 32, 33

reed boats 24, 25
remedies 39
roads 26–27

sacrifice, human 5, 36
Serpent Mound 12, 13
silver 34–35
slipware 42
smallpox 39
solstices 23, 29
Sonoran Desert 11
Southwest 4, 16–17, 20
Spaniards 4, 5, 34, 37
surgery 39

technological background 6–7
Tenochtitlán 15, 20–21, 25, 29
Teotihuacán 7, 15
terraces 10–11
textiles 40–41
Toltec 7
transportation 24–25

warfare 36–37
weapons 36–37
wheel 24, 25, 26
wool 41
writing 32–33